Femme's Dictionary

by
Carol Guess

CALYX Books • Corvallis, Oregon

Publication of this book is supported in part by a grant from the Oregon Cultural Trust, investing in Oregon's arts, humanities, and heritage; The Rose Tucker Charitable Trust; and the generous support of an anonymous donor.

Cover art and author photo by Joanne Tilley
Cover and book design by Cheryl McLean

CALYX Books are distributed to the trade through Consortium Book Sales and Distribution, Inc., St. Paul, MN, 1-800-283-3572.

CALYX Books are also available through major library distributors, jobbers, and most small press distributors including Airlift, Baker & Taylor, Ingram, and Small Press Distribution. For personal orders or other information contact: CALYX Books, PO Box B, Corvallis, OR 97339, (541) 753-9384, Fax (541) 753-0515, E-mail: calyx@proaxis.com.

∞

The paper in this book meets the guidelines for permanence and durability of the Committee on Production Guidelines for Book Longevity of the Council on Library Resources and the minimum requirements of the American National Standard for the Permanence of Paper for Printed Library Materials Z38.48-1984.

Library of Congress Cataloging-in-Publication Data
Guess, Carol.
  Femme's dictionary / by Carol Guess.
    p. cm.
  ISBN 0-934971-86-2 (pbk. : alk. paper) – ISBN 0-934971-87-0 (cloth (lib bdg) : alk. paper)
1. Women—Poetry. I. Title.

PS3557.U3438F46 2004
811'.54—dc22   2004017004

Printed in the U.S.A.   9 8 7 6 5 4 3 2 1

Acknowledgments

I'm grateful to the amazing folks at CALYX Books for putting so much time and care into this volume. Special thanks to Margarita Donnelly, Alice Ann Eberman, Beverly McFarland, and Micki Reaman for devoted editing and publication detail.

Special thanks to my family—Ali, Mom, and Dad—with my deepest love and gratitude.

Thanks to Jackie Fiegel, Kathryn Stevenson, and Lola Waters for making a home with me during the war. I'm grateful to the friends and fellow poets who let me bounce ideas back and forth: Gwendolyn Bikis, Deb Lantz, Mandy Laughtland, Leslie Leasure, Tonia Matthew, and Kerry Maddox Regan. To Ely and Rainer for companionship. To Kathleen Kennedy for sweetness and faith. To Samantha Bennett for opening the orange curtains. To Nichola Torbett for underground river rides. To Joanne Tilley for lap dances, cover art, and intuition. To Sandy Yannone, always, for everything.

Many of the poems in this collection were originally published, some in slightly different forms, in the following publications: *Bakunin, Bay Windows, CAIRN, Crab Orchard Review, Cranky, Epicenter, The Gay and Lesbian Review, Gerbil, Hiram Poetry Review, Icon, Illya's Honey, Interim, The Jabberwock Review, Mankato Poetry Review, Natural Bridge, No Exit, Poetry Motel, Poetry Northwest*, and *Red Cedar Review*.

Special thanks to the following publishers and writers for permission to reprint words from: "Violence, Mourning, Politics" by Judith Butler, in *Queer Ideas*, published by The Feminist Press at City University of New York; *Cool for You* by Eileen Myles, published by Soft Skull Press; "The Girl Who Catches Everything" by Sandra Yannone, published by *Prairie Schooner*, University of Nebraska Press; "Baby Doll" by JT Leroy, in *The Heart Is Deceitful Above All Things*, published by Bloomsbury USA.

for Sandy Yannone, who read it first
for Nichola Torbett, who encouraged me to finish it
for Joanne Tilley, who opened it carefully

Femme's Dictionary

III

IV

Aperture

In a photograph taken when I was two, I'm sitting in the drawer of a filing cabinet, playing with my toes. A dog-eared sticker on the front of the drawer reads *Radioactive* and I am, I glow. I glow blonde, white-blonde, sun-slashed, contented. I am a West Coast baby sitting in a filing cabinet marked *Radioactive*, waiting on a difficult father who scrawls numbers in chalk. He, in turn, is waiting on a difficult admiral to tell him whether some submarine will sink or swim.

Days, my father feeds cards into a computer the size of our home, cards he carries home for me to color. Nights, I do not have a sister and I do not dream of the sister I'll have. Oh, the years without her, the time when I am the center of two beautiful, terrible attention spans! My father vanishes, returns, vanishes again. He begins to make numbers mean important things.

I am two. I am almost a Christmas baby, almost a tax break. My sister is not yet born, not yet conceived. When she is born, she will take over, occupying space with miniature authority, a lazy ease passersby will call *adorable*. I will be bald, still. Mistaken for a boy. I will bypass *adorable* and go straight to *clever*.

Later, when my mother feeds me fish, I will spit it out and stuff it in my sister's mouth.

But just then I am glowing, radioactive. My father is watching a sub fill with water. My mother is not ready for her father to die.

Most beautiful is my mother in photos with cats, her thick black eyeliner incautiously feline. I am the one with the Cheshire smile—at two, even.

My father frowns.

My sister is not yet born.

When they play Muzak at the naval base, the admiral sends out a call. A phone rings. Doors slam. A messenger appears out of nowhere, sprinting. Rips out the speaker above each door on the hall.

(Years later, during a fight over gays in the military: *Those submarines,* my father says, *are very small.*)

But I'm not yet gay. I love only my toes, and my difficult father, and my porcelain mother. At night my father vanishes, or goes stone, or plays Linda Ronstadt, The Beatles, and Elton John: *Rock me on the ramble, Rocket Man. Lucy in the wings with the walrus hammer.*

I love my parents and they love me. I wear pink flowery nightgowns, although my mother later erases this memory, finding it easier to remember her dyke daughter in PJs. I name our first cat after my favorite food: spaghetti with meatballs. And our second cat after my second favorite: spaghetti with meatballs. They become Meatballs One and Meatballs Two, then One and Two, then *was* and *were*.

By then I have a sister. And she is more beautiful than I, ahead of me already, and she thinks this of me, and so we learn to hate women.

❦

But that's not the story I meant to tell. The story I meant to tell has no beginning and no end and runs underneath the story of my sister like a river. My father hovers in the aperture of a glistening window, suicide botched by his mother's ghost. Numbers from his slide rule pause on the sill, fallen by chance into a brilliant formula.

My mother walks to school in a flour sack printed with pansies, her German accent smeared with eggs. Her last name means *graveyard circled with trees*. Verbs dawdle between the gaps in her teeth.

My parents, speaking German in a German cafe, capitalizing every noun carefully, making new words from old, homesick at last. My parents in Heidelberg, only not yet my parents. Harold Adelbert, meet Geraldine Ann. She's shy, her hands covering uneven teeth. He's an engineer geek: highwaters, pocket protector. Both speak fluently but neither fools the other. American-born, they'll return to different worlds. After Heidelberg their courtship is epistolary, a literary romance I'll never read. Geraldine's father Stanley burns their love letters. *Ravish.* Oh mother! *Your slender hands.*

And she becomes a navy wife.

And he thinks he's finally escaped the South.

And she hopes someday to become middle class.

And he becomes acquainted with great tenderness.

During Vietnam he works at Naval Reactors among a tight-knit, top-secret gaggle of math majors. He helps design nuclear submarines, the first of many dramatic careers. So much to discover, so many numbers to love! His brief forays away from theory end in dismay as he encounters humans.

But numbers and power, the great nuclear mystery. I am born to a genius no one can take anywhere, who scrawls formulas on tablecloths in fancy restaurants and doesn't look either way when crossing the street. Occasionally he forgets his address and thumbs through the phone book to call home and ask.

My mother manages him; this becomes her career. Over the years she learns piles of secrets. Discoveries yield to her as she tends to their maker. She arranges father, business, and us.

Carol Ann, meet Alison Pauline.

In pictures I hate her. They've obviously made me hold her; I'm posed like a doll. My sister's face lolls up at me, happy. She's always drooling; my eyes look crazed.

And I think she's more beautiful.

And she thinks I'm ahead.

And I long for the *friend* my mother promised.

And she's shamed by my difference: *freak, slut, queer.*

No one should have a sibling. What an impossible relation, an arranged marriage, maybe worse. This person, your blood, no one you've chosen.

And we want to love each other.

And we try until it turns to rage.

Little Trimesters, little sisters. Two girls, unlucky, stars burning too brightly. Strange family, with a hole at its center. I am trying to make sense of my distant father. *Very good, Carol. Carol, be still.* At school I'm already becoming the sea.

Shy girl to whom numbers mean nothing. Holding the clock to my forehead, my tongue. Unable to match minutes to hours. Dreaming already, little poems about ghosts.

My sister flits past me, grown-up already. Boys like a beacon in her version of night. I slide through the holes in my parents' stories, past the blue before speech to which I try to return.

I

I think that if I can still speak to a "we," or include myself within its terms, I am speaking to those of us who are living in certain ways beside ourselves, *whether it is in sexual passion, or emotional grief, or political rage.*
Judith Butler, "Violence, Mourning, Politics"

Watercolor: Leda

The swan nestles his beak between the woman's
smallish breasts. His wings curve like orchards
or the broad flaps of planes that seared
acres of sky in the early months
of the last noticeable war. Returning
from the front, a man lays his head
between his lover's breasts, listening
for the heart nestled among orchards of skin and bone.
He lets scars drift from him like petals.
He pretends he can forget acres of names.

The most noticeable thing in the picture
is the quiet of the woman's lips
as the bird comes to her, and she pretends
she will forget warm breath to breast,
beast-touch. But everything returns to haunt,
like obscene pictures, like the heart
of the swan, beating a rhythm out
beneath winged ribs. The murmur of push or drop
through the bird's heart flaps, the murmur
of beautiful, dead men in their last flights returns,

and it is like the return
of the planes at night, when someone's war
has just begun to drop. The soldier lets his thoughts
nestle among the rhythms of the early front. The woman
rests her forehead between wingspread hands,
and the old hopes drift like petals
shaken from boughs in pre-war orchards,
before the great planes seared their trunks
with scars, obscenely small, like names.

The Driven

Small houses bracket the great cities. In those outskirts
we're born, riding out on the pain of a woman's open body.
We die crumpling among seed packets and garden gloves
in dusk, at seventy. The suburbs create us. If we escape, it's to ride
trains we can't trust underground, looking for money. Losing sleep
over women. I told my father I was leaving; I was seventeen.
His face crumpled. I told him I was losing sleep
over a woman and his dusky eyes closed.

We bracket our parents' lives. We want them
secure in small houses, reading and gardening, drinking
warm things from scalloped glasses. How difficult it is
to imagine them gone, or in pain. How difficult
to imagine anything at all, when I am sleeping

in a house in the suburbs where ambition dries like water
on concrete terraces. I told my father a story;
he was half asleep on the scalloped sofa. Dusk
covered half his face, and for a moment I felt afraid.
I touched his arm, just to be sure. He asked me to read
to him, to bring him something warm to drink, and to be sure
never to leave the suburbs. I promised something,

but rain drove me out of terraced gardens and I woke
on a warm train that filled great cities
with the young ambitious. I drank in their stories:
face after face untouchable, but open. The eyes of one man
were bracketed by shadow. He stretched the train's length,
shaded his face, slept. The ride curved on, as if
it trusted him. From underneath his palms came weeping.
The sound reminded me of rain.

Don't Ask, Don't Tell

When you sleep with a gun for the first time,
you interrogate its history like any lover's,
imagining the deaths it holds in store. When you wed,
the world welcomes your union. Your children's cries
drag the country in the wake of their echoes.

When the gun goes off, you hold water in your hands.
It moves gracefully through your fingers
as the body you've signed becomes a photograph.
Tell no one, another soldier murmurs
as he too takes aim. You breathe and march in unison,

feet stirring the same dry clay into the same dusty spirals.
The songs you exhale make of women the enemy,
their breasts landing sites, their legs
stone columns you must weave your way between.
Nights, you sleep below him on a metal cot

that rocks backwards like a train. *Promise*, he says,
but he is talking in his sleep, his boyish voice contorted
by the remnants of compassion. The force of his solitude
reaches you through plaited wire. If you reached for him . . .
But your relation is merely political.

Don't ask, croons your superior, and reason wavers,
hazy as a target in stark desert sun. But you have a question.
You want to ask what love is, if this is love:
what you feel when anonymous blood runs swiftly,
drizzled in fitful patterns like festive stars.

Bad Sex

Everything tousled, and then the end zone:
that lie you started things off with
haunts us yet. You shrink from my hands
as I become your father;
the TV flies towards the wall
and I'm wholly new, a violent,
desiring man. Meanwhile, in my reality,
your breasts are in my hands,
we're women overcoming history,
I'm in bliss not wholly new,
violently unaware
that you're not there.

Now you're not here:
two hundred miles by interstate.
I write and call to say I miss
what you don't think we had at all.
But if that's all, whose hands
did I inhabit when I touched
the deer-brown curve of clavicle
that clothed your pulse? Which ghost
pinned both my hands above my head
and bit down hard, trying to reach
its history through my flesh?
I couldn't separate your love
from my discomfort; you couldn't separate
my fierce desire from walking,
evenings, through flooded woods
beside your father. His old brown coat.
Pressing your knee against my throat:
what life in your eyes as you re-live
the trip to the river. I just shiver,
liking the perfume of angry breath.

Femme's Dictionary

She says she wore a dress that first Saturday,
but I say, *Skirt, skirt,*
insistence darkening my lips
as if the difference
between cloth or a zipper at her waist
might've held us together longer.

I like to call things by their names.
I like to make my words match,
as much as possible,
the thoughts I'm holding onto.
Not love, but *a stranger's hand
in my jacket pocket.* Not *aquamarine,*
but *the color of blood
between a woman's thighs.*

She was different from me.
She enjoyed lying,
the way a hand touching the surface of the water
enjoys the water: its frail and fleeting clasp.
What is it makes impermanence so sensuous?

She liked to watch
me leave, needing the sound of a door
to remind her of where my lips had lingered.
Not *bedroom* but *vestibule,*
nine letters to describe the space
she cleared for me. Not quite a room.

Which One of You Is the Man?

The flecked eye of a fish is a window;
the gaze of a cow edging the ramp to slaughter
is a gun. Is sap the same as blood? What I long for
is to see inside the hearts of things and not
incorporate them. I've seen a tie undo itself
because it felt the pulse of her throat
and admired the precarious math of human life.
I want to hear in the jutting of car alarms
the music of urban proximity. When I say, *Take me,*
I mean for my body to tell stories about night,
how it feels when the moon strokes its belly.
What I long for are wrists that know enough
to stay away from razors. Which one of us lies
on top of the other, steering until pleasure
feels simple, because detached from choice?
In the grocery, those rows of hearts might be
human, altering forever the meaning of desire.

But You Two Girls Don't Have the Right Equipment

*That which withers in the age of mechanical
reproduction,* wrote Walter Benjamin, *is the aura
of the work of art.* As I paint this picture
along your back, I see anew the sloped wings
hidden beneath slick olive skin. Love,
what snowflake pattern will you shimmer in
when we bed down? Around us, neighbors stack
beautiful cups in the corners of crowded houses,
filling their mouths with salt, once precious.
The drone of breakfasts and children's
guns resounds, prelude to no first movement.
And there is no movement on this block, no motion
forward or back, but only upwards to a man-made
heaven. Love, it's too simple to mimic;
I'm giving my breath away in a song invented
for this moment, nothing to keep or copy.
I want you to see me handmade, to know the tips
of my fingers, purple and chapped, nothing
beautiful. I won't buy you a sweater but split open
my chest, trusting the heat of an authentic gesture.
Outside, a miniature tractor turns snowflakes
into slush. Children tread cautiously, guns clasped
close, unused to dropping to their knees, bedding
together, shimmering a frozen ocean into angels.

Public Sex

The Vintage Garage is open till ten—
better than a movie. We skip women's, head straight
for men's more comfortable, looser fits.
When something's muted, we devour it.
This is heaven: you modeling a suit for me
behind a flimsy partition marked with a heel.
Here's where our ambiguous status reveals
itself, murky as your skin in fluorescent light.
We can walk boldly together, or vanish,
seams of the same dress; we're bound
one minute, free the next. Invisibility
yields safety, but also hopelessness,
a twentieth-century Pandora scraping
a voided trunk. You discard your coat;
your sex is warm as a rabbit's open
throat. These small deaths, beautiful
and terrible, remake us, till all we are,
some days, is what we know
no one sees. When we emerge, arms laden
with ten dollars' worth of purchases, you're
a man again. I take your arm. The cashier
calls me *Missy*, and if nothing is missing
at that moment, who can blame us?

This must be how old clothes feel, passing
endlessly from one life to the next.
Home again, your answering machine adds
to the layering—another banal convo,
another misuse of *friend*, my new
least favorite word. Ah, love, let us be true
to choice, as true to her as she is to us,
allowing her the courtesy of struggle,
attempting at least to top her, the way
old-fashioned femmes at least pretended
to resist. *It's an obligation,* I say; you say,
A gift. You're arranging restless silk,
sheer cotton, paint-stained corduroy;
you're an artist in your narrow closet,
and when you reach for me, I forget politics,
I give in, I become who I am. How many wars
were lost this way: tongue to hip, hopelessness
transmuted into lust? If only it were easier
to always be us; if only this starry room
were beach, river, city; if only I could kiss
your thighs and call it making history.

Stealing Peonies

You have a knife; open their gate.
Startle me with what I know is free.
When your chest is wet
with the slash and split of blossoms
wide as neighbors' wakeful eyes, whistle me in.
I'll climb the fence to where you hijink,
waist-high in fuchsia buds and blooms.

Back home, dump wooden spoons from a vase,
fool the flowers with water,
and fold the knife, which you've forgotten,
into your pocket: a robber's hand.
Admire the peonies in silence,
afraid to break the brilliance of one sense
to feed another. Flood the curtains
with red reflections; the petals will light the room,
brittle, descend, finally die.

By then, you and I will be speaking again,
women's words settling like dust
among everyday senses. By then, sight
will function simply for direction; beauty,
a luxury not viewed as a friend.
When you whistle me in,
the notes will blend with bleating trucks
and sparrows' storm warnings.
But all red remains a reminder:
when we bleed, we steal time together.

That Gift You Gave Me

A sweet skirt surrounds the vase of the peonies
you stole for me. Which is more beautiful:
cut flowers, stiff in their urge for sustenance,
or dried petals, scattered in a solemn ring?
Like everything we've asked each other, the answer
is none of the above. I remember the living flowers,
blossoming because they had no audience, startled
by unsought human hands. I remember the knife,
and the water on your wrists, and the wind
billowing your blouse as you rushed back to me.
What if someone had seen us? They'd know we took
live things, let them fade, called it *pleasure*.
Today I watch the petals drift onto the pale pine table
and listen for your call, which doesn't come, and doesn't,
as if you can see, from the faraway you've chosen,
the phone cord coiled like snakeskin, shaken off.

But the Weather

Because she isn't speaking, you turn your head
towards the oleander. Cars drag blue dust and music.
The factory's siding gleams; inside, appliances
—accomplished, slick—ride the conveyor.
She's waiting for you to speak. But the weather
swings like the cat's toy pendulum, and the cat
sings to itself: *good night, good night,* though
it's noon, clasped flowers relaxing in the palm
of the grass. You drum your fingers on the hood.
Last night a cop sat poised in the factory lot
timing traffic, cupping his mike to his lips, kiss
like the oleander's staticky blossoms: buzzing,
keeping watch. Because she isn't speaking,
you examine grey asphalt speckling yellow
stripes. The sky mottles. Then the sound
of Puccini, tossed like a coin from a speeding car.

The Place I Let You Go

The day the mountain crumbled
you changed your name
to the name of the woman
who crossed the border and back again.
A little death here, a little burial there,
and anyway the birds dot the urban foliage
of orange cranes sipping beach water,
dredging boxcars up from the dead.

Sometimes something broken
can't be mended. A man fell asleep
in a vat at the steel mill off Avalon Way.
What they poured over him made him stronger
as the dead do for the living
having done what none of us can.

Pouring down like sand
the mountain revises our history—
rubble everywhere
as if we'd been any good at shaking.
Death missed me, poured over him,
steeling the men who witnessed the mystery.
Who am I to release you
as you released the dead in bed with me?
In the place I let you go
you'll rise like smoke from my lips
burning invisible inside me.

Ample

Erase rain; erase the opposite of rain.
This house stands stark
against no weather. Whether or not
to love again, that's my question.

The doe knows. She comes and goes, rejecting
carrots, wary of the dog's cold kisses
and the cat's half-moles—love
letters, every broken bone.

She knows what daylight keeps, and night.
She saw the lights go off, heard
what came after: laughter, shared
by weathered women. She doesn't care.

She doesn't care for humankind,
wishes the highway knew its place.
She doesn't pace for love or lust,
but tramps her luck in skittish grass.

I picture you ten years from now, ample
still, unspent by men. And me?
I see myself in this queer house,
the lights relaxed, not out but dim,

knowing I had everything, and the doe
still coming, and my own slow pulse,
and weeds. I can see me, finger
to the lips you bent to kiss,

that half-step back.
I'd take it back.
But time is weather—fickle, proud.
The doe retreats. The highway's loud.

Bonfire

Now that the smoke from photos, letters,
and your blue cotton sweater has passed
through wind to become wind; now that fire
has passed through red, orange, and grey,
and the ground where I stacked sticks
has been raked over and over, the way you raked
my face with lashes that never blinked;
now that sunset has no competition,
and the view from my window is once more
a garden; now that I own nothing
to remind me, I find arson's erasure
an inverted failure. Once, trinkets were all;
now all that exists stands witness—
the scent of your hair is wind, the taste
of your blood is salt, your silhouette
crouches in every tree, and the ecstasy
of our rained kisses, mist. My guess:
you don't miss me, yet I can't inhabit
a world that isn't also your body.
I remember you touching coils
of moss, tasting mint, thinking of things
in themselves, dismissing anthropopathism.
Now I plant bulbs in a plot of raked ash,
giving each blossom the same woman's name.

Last

Cars shiver past like ice shaken from a tray;
your words chisel my features
till I resemble your father. Cruelty becomes us.
We hurt each other because it's natural,
and because it's taught, each lesson tinted
to correspond to a particular season.
Tonight it's snow. The clock on the nightstand
ticks *sorry, sorry* as if it too were airborne water
meeting earth. Our mouths open to something
that resembles a kiss, but tastes of aftermath.
That look of panic returns to your fingertips,
your hair swallows your eyes, you take my face
between your palms and turn my gaze away.
If this dun house had windows, passersby
could watch grown women fumbling
with the clothes that make them masochists.
You hand back the hand I gave in bedside darkness,
calling me by the name I'd said was mine.

II

I wanted to go home, where I had never been.
Eileen Myles, *Cool For You*

Five

What I remember of being dizzy: the smell
of shaving cream, the bug-studded glass
over the ceiling bulb I could almost touch.
One arm beneath my legs, the other under
my narrow shoulders: me in his arms,
a backwards *C*, I'm giggling, my father's humming
something seventies, gritty as the light
scraping the kitchen curtains. The clock
is blurry, and my hair, swinging
as my head drops back, as my father turns,
slowly at first, then faster, spinning
till we're both too dizzy and he stops
dead and I keen, not mourning but wanting more,
my mouth open in pleasure, my father
staggering a little. The two of us
blink, seeing double. The room unwinds.
The clock ticks into focus, unstoppable.

Median

Most fatal accidents happen close to home.
My grandparents tucked their car tight
around suburban corners
until a drunk driver jumped the median.

Most suburban hazards have names like *neighbor*.
I was fifteen. He knew my name.
He tucked me in while my parents travelled.
They were orphans by then, and accidents happen.

In the suburbs drunk drivers are an occupational hazard.
Boys burned rubber. My neighbor cruised
my ribs, easy to count through no accident
but the suburban occupation of starvation.

Good fences, said Frost. On standardized tests
I learned that *sex* is to *rape* as *merge* is to *median*.
My sex was an accident: they wanted a son.
Who would I be if I'd stayed close to home?

Post

I wrote my sister a letter in a swirling hand.
The paper was beautiful: sheer, burnt-cream lapped
edges. I gave a warning. I said that things
had changed, and to hurry back. I said write back,

but between the lines was an edge of irony, dark
as ink, meant to burn. My sister's letter
never came. Instead, an envelope from overseas
with beautiful stamps and sheer, hurried pen strokes

fell through the slot, warning me
that people I will never see exist, and are aware
of irony. I wrote back, copied the beautiful address
in a dark, back-slanted hand onto an envelope

that once held seeds. The sides were pockmarked;
it smelled of moss and burning leaves. Inside
was nothing but a sheet of paper asking someone
to write back. Warning them that I existed.

A slot accepted the letter as if it were nothing,
sent it overseas without asking questions or burning
its moss-green edges. It was a lesson in irony, but
beautiful, smelling of change, of hands working

to sort seed packets from sheets of newsprint.
I couldn't see the hands, but knew they touched
my letter lightly, as if it burned,
then sent it swirling on its way, without warning.

My Hands My Camera

My mother in the snapshot
cancer causes.
My hands my camera
as I shell her pills.
My mother waiting
for me to swell
with witness. She wishes.
Writing on the wall
between us. Me in bed
with someone's breasts.
My chest the negative
of the next thirty years.
Developing my mother's
features. Our fracture.
My mother in hospital
without me inside her.

Kiosk

My sister sent me a photograph. Standing
before a signpost, holding the gloved
hand of a dark-haired woman, my sister's smile
is like graffiti: assertive, indecipherable.
Two bicycles rest against a battered kiosk.
Her feet are splayed: a dancer's first.
I sent news, and this is what it got me:
A'dam-Noord, two women, gloves, a graffitied
kiosk. The dark-haired woman signed the photograph.
I wonder where my sister got her, how many
dances it took, if she was the first, or if the color
on my sister's cheeks is from the cold.
I understand nothing of how she got there.
Perhaps we aren't sisters, just cousins
with identical hands and darkening hair.
She used to dance; I rode balloons into the cold
night air above stiff signposts. She used to speak,
but now she signs, and sends words tied
to posts: A'dam-Noord, a name I can't pronounce,
through black graffiti barely visible.

Answering Back

My sister calls, all concerned
because her hair is orange. I try to muster
sympathy, but can't, the way I can't feel anything
for the guy in aerobics who keeps tripping
over his Step. She reads me the contents
of the bottle. Her words take shape, brighten
and loosen, then dissolve. I think I was seven
before I realized my mother's accent changed
to match other people's voices. I see
my sister's face, framed by red frizz.
She's saying something about *origins*.
She's out there searching for an anodyne.
I do a dance to the phone's static: first
flailing arms, and then the tangle.
I see my mother, drinking it black
because the guests do. I was seventeen
before I knew she wanted sugar.
What makes me wonder is what keeps him
coming back, only to spill, again, somebody's
bottled water: each time the same tsunami.
My sister's trying to eliminate dark roots.
To lose her accent: breathy tangle of cast-off
voices, simply dissolved, sugar in water.

Cotillion

The young girls dance like leaves,
or dogs eager for supper:
rustle and sparkle, winter and sweat.
This moment is crucial.
Boys turn them this way and that;
the couples practice, practice,
until they become their parents.

Beyond the ballroom, in the bathroom's
inner sanctum, two wallflowers
comb their hair with ruthless vigor,
dresses ripped beneath the arms.
Their glances flicker shyly, as if the glass cared
what their curls did. As if the boys did.

Inside the ballroom, stars bristle red;
music floats gratuitously overhead.
Over the whirling couples' heads are hung
a silver sun and moon. It's too soon
for rings; each girl's bare fingers sparkle,
pink and amber lacquer long enough to scratch
the line of skin above a beau's stiff collar,
waiting for the crisp sucking-in of breath
when he's surprised by touch, pleased or put off.

The wallflowers hardly miss the scratches
and after-kisses. They've coaxed a gaza
away from sinks and stalls: the make-up room
has loveseats and its door shuts neatly;
peach walls glimmer, a trellised pattern.
They share secrets, narrating the kisses

that will rouse them, never imagining
who will really touch them. The room's a closet,
but they call it heaven-haven, forgetting
the why of when they came. Their talk
stirs breezes; though the walls are windowless,
they know what color sky it is.

The Idea of Kid

When I run, I pass a place that has a kid.
The facade is stoic brick, the grass
snipped close to stubble, but the narrow window
on the east side gives it away: blue sheep
and fat gold stars pasted recklessly
along the inner glass. Sure enough,
one morning there's a woman in a robe,
holding in her arms this thing she's talking to.
I can imagine: braving frost in a fuzzy wrap,
talking aloud. But not holding something
that was once practically a limb.

Of course, I've taken care of shy
and rowdy kids; perhaps *Where's Waldo?*
means more when the kid is yours. But maybe not:
I'm impatient with everything; I like my dinner
hot and early; I'm surly often; often, I give in
too easily. I look in other people's windows;
when I see something that intrigues me, stop.
Like the window with the sheep: up
close, before the bushes but beyond the curb,
crib bars emerge, and the kid's black sort-of-hair.
I admit it's cute; though I dislike sentimentality,
still, its face is shades away from blue. It breathes
ambitiously; if it's lucky, the breath it turns
to cries will become words. Kid'll wake up
asking for stuff. That I can imagine:
speaking to someone, getting a reply.

Unnatural Passions

All lines lead to your daughter: this scrap of paper,
this shard of history swirl until they settle,
web more than cloak. We stare at the clock.
Something's happened, irrevocable. Our slick mouths
leave her vulnerable to a court as brutal and relentless
as paternity. Her curiosity fuels her days; we bear its scrutiny.
You assume she wants secrets exposed, your body seen
in its reality: more than mother, hungry woman. Lover.
But that's bright, and what your daughter notices
are shadows. At nine, she knows the thing you and I
were late to see: that there are those who would take her
simply because they can. Can we blame her, having lived
as gentle women all our lives, under men's shadows,
if it's their power she's curious after, and not the glint
of our bodies together, wound round in pleasure,
synchronicity beyond power? At nine, she knows
it's the man down the chimney, the woman who sets out
milk. She knows her surname, Scottish as your ex-husband's
tweeds. Can we blame her for learning ordinary lessons?
The whole world's waiting for this girl to bleed.

Daywatch

Mornings, I take the dog to the park
when the grass is wet still, and cool:
six o'clock, sun meets hill, scattering light
on the figures in green and brown
belly-down on the lawn, rustling.
The ROTC crowd.

The greeny men
murmur to each other
like lovers.

Once, the dog tugged loose,
circled the park.
Though I tired of running after,
she just went faster.

My lover's heart beats faster
as she wakes to find me missing.
What circles never stops:
the men drop to their knees,
the sun describes the park,
I double-cross the man-made river.
There's something I haven't told her.

Five soldiers form a cross; dog runs
her tongue along damp grass.
I watch sun glinting off the open blades.

Lament for the Last Man

Which one of us has the wrong body?
In my dreams you become a woman.
The unused flesh falls away,
singing dust. I put my mouth to the new wound,
drink the liquid that leaves us childless.

When you dream, what do I become?
Woman of windows, woman
of doors, each unlocked clasp
a tiny sigh: *surfaces, surfaces!*

You wake to my impenetrable circle.
I wake into my skin, wrap it tighter.
If only our bodies understood what we long for.

Adultery Is Easy

Gravity makes no sound.
The pull happens on its own.
We know nothing of our bodies
outside that force,

alive in us, compelling us
to fall towards things we love,
things that never rise
to catch, never weave nets.

I can easily imagine the sound of her hair
as you sucked the ends,
so thirsty, unaware
of what was and wasn't water.

Allegro Barbaro

Clouds strike the sky till rain sparks, a curtain
of silver fire. Your body brings the window closer,
rain wanting in to hear what I do: hands measuring
keys, so purposeful you forget I'm watching. I do too.
But later, I'll know I'm watching you
bent over me, overhang, your small eye tearing,
my breasts a cavern for something swarming.

If you had a different body, I might keep you,
tucked as women once were—in a kitchen
the size of a closet, or tugging roots in a garden
where rain illuminates rough-fisted roses.
That's what I fear: that I would make that sort
of a man. But I am a woman, and between us
lies fire, drawn curtains, a tossed glove.

The score shivers, melody lost. What's left
is something brash, blinding me, as I wish to be blinded,
to the awful mystery of how things are made.
Sound connects us; sound, and the gestures
you make to cull it, and the poise of my listening
to keep it: music sticky as spider's lace,
not a gamble but a fisted ace. Last week, wind

stroked a woman's curtains, accompanying my breath
as I slept beside her. She touched me once;
the difference between us made loss inevitable.
Things happened, the way things happen when you and I
are in a room, but her hands refused keys, and her eyes
saw through me. If I speak sometimes of *longing,*
this is what I mean: nothing is simple.

Bartok knew this also. No clarity, no beauty,
nothing but courage to create intensity. Both of us
want a woman's body. If I cover your eyes
with my hands, will the notes go on, rough
as the work we do to stay together?
Will your body matter? Mine is not enough.

Writing Desire

After she left, he remained in motion:
a hanging plant, twisting.
He said the word *desire*.
He tried to write *desire*
on a wall beside a window
with his palm, a kitchen knife, a pillow.

How he'd carved space for her!
As one carves pumpkins for children:
the quick incision, everything jagged, gutting.
Now the shell, candleless;
the open mouth unsmiling,
wrinkling in its after-season.

What he wouldn't give her
was loneliness. His four walls grew
to look too much like hands. Writing *desire,*
he sees what she saw:
the faint outline of cupped palms,
their lifelines curving.

III

In the future, twirling

naked in bed, we will remember these girls
we did not have the chance to undress
when we had all the time in the world.
            Sandra Yannone, "The Girl Who
                Catches Everything"

Misanthropy

Can a soul be autistic? Love knocks, and I recoil.
This morning the world comes to me, soft; I say,
Carry me in your mouth. The trees bend to whisper,
and the sparrows, basking in last night's crumbs,
tell me, *You must learn to speak again.* Every morning
I wake from dreams in which I finally connect
with other people—care to—into the blood-
orange sunlight of solitude, and the knowledge that I don't.
Yet I envy proximity. Each blade of grass learns
the same story, memorizes roots, a slow-motion
thrust for survival. Dickinson was right: *just a turn—*
and freedom, Matty! I haven't the excuse of a corset,
muzzle; people just puzzle me. The realm of fantasy's
more familiar than any lover's breath. How many of us?
Or is it cold comfort to count, knowing none will seek
the others out? Ghostie, come to me. Let me whisper
a story, a tragedy: how much this lady (yet lonely) hated
human hands. How Bell invented the telephone,
and later, whoever-the-hell invented the fax just for her.
Be my salvation: composite of old wives and imagined
spirits, alive in memory only, beyond frowns, denial, debt.
Ghostie, if you are sky, zoom in; gown me in clouds
draped like a shroud: miracle of no saint, only a nerdy
sleeper whose hands shattered hearts. Gown me, Ghostie.
Clue me in to the secret of the haunting you do, do best;
teach me how to live alone and yet be blessed.

Still Life with Lap Dog

The room's blue. She waits for me to finish sleeping.
When I creak from bed, she needs to eat.

Years pass.

I care for her much the way I care for myself.
There's a dish with multicolored food, there's water.
We walk four times a day: a sloppy circle.
Sometimes, special, I clean her teeth.

Her breath reminds me of her fur.
She's wet when it rains, and wet when she bites
the fleas that cluster in camps on her belly.
She licks my cheek to rinse away stale ash.

Nights, she yawns, and I see how pink her tongue,
how black her velvety inner lips, flopping over
their ruffled outer edges. Her tails sags like a sack.

She pools at my feet to sleep, and forgets my life for me.

What hasn't happened

yet lingers, like our parents' hold on heaven,
or the urge to apologize for wearing men's clothes.
Above our heads, husky songs spiral;
at the window, a spider sews your curtains shut.
Close your eyes, you tell me,
but candles parody some real surprise. I want you
to startle me with something other than smoke,
something ephemeral, but tailored to another sense.
In your closet: suit jackets, a trunk full of ties.
If in some album, this moment becomes a prelude
rather than a continuum, I promise, mornings,
to ease the silk gently around your throat,
leaving it to you to tug the knot. I promise—
but I'll stop. Nothing your hands or eyes have done
gives me license to make you my new religion.
That's what they bet on. We're different,
or so we say, from parents who eked lives out
the old way, parents who waltzed
or waded down a long red aisle, one in white,
one in black, making that distinction into a living map.
We're different—so different we sit here waiting,
instead of turning to each other, saying, *Darling,
this is how it's done.* Neither of us wants
to be the one to start or finish things off,
so we sit, trying not to touch,
enumerating to each other all the *whys*
of women who've too long refused to compromise.

A Brief History of the Pay Phone

Six hours from where I should be, I join a line
of refugees, escaped convicts, and sentimental lovers
outside an old-fashioned booth. Some het girl's
engagement glints against blue dusk,
refracting heartfelt Midwestern advertising—
dinosaur-shaped burgers. What neon wants
is for the sky to bear her slash. What I want
is to fathom cow emotions: bleating and bleating,
begging for mercy, knowing not one syllable
will filter through. I squat on the curb, hugging
my knees to my heart, knowing nothing
my mother taught me has prepared me
for this woman's hands. The glass door skids open;
a cape whisks off. I wind my watch, waiting
for the coffee to kick in and the cows to rise up,
angry and very beautiful, great spots blossoming
across their bellies, as if scarring their hearts
against human hunger. The sliding door creases,
losing its scenery; trucks drown out the yammer
of obsolete coins. I'm here to tell her
that she has her mother's hands, that caffeine
is a poor substitute for heartfelt emotion,
and that passion has chosen the circle
for its shape. I give her a ring. I give her another.

They coil around her dog's sleeping body, the thick
hearts of her wrists, and her neutral clock.
What does it mean to trust sound siphoned through
alphabets we can't decipher? If she picks up,
her stories will be parables; my gestures choreographed,
Midwestern-cautious, each shake of luscious
Jell-O carefully planned. I'm here to tell her
what women must teach each other: sentimentality
is an art. I want to show her the way the silver lines
of her lashes and the sliver of red beneath her heavy
breasts become magic pencils that never need
sharpening. The ringing inspires me; I conduct
frantically, gaining and losing control
of distant orchestration. I imagine filling her house
with sound, spending everything I've ever earned
in one night's orgy of ceaseless yammering,
tattooing my ear forever with the tell-tale welts
of long-distance affection. I hang up. I hang my head.
I hang onto the door as it opens, taking me for a tiny ride.

What Your Parents Don't Know

Here's an album. Fill it with photographs:
adorable white children, immaculate lawns,
sloe-eyed pets. Hug the album to your chest—
the blank pages are photographs of me.
At nineteen, although we haven't met,
starve yourself so your breasts won't stir me.
Perfect field hockey; spend weekends drinking
from a hip flask in the library. Travel
restlessly. Fuck men with a jaded expression
several will mistake for passion. Now meet me.
Now adore me.
Now ask me—*a close friend*—to visit
Hotel Purgatory in Connecticut. Remind me
to leave my toy collection in the closet.

It was you who alerted me to the sadness
of airports: all that emotion poised for take-off.
I've hidden my desire in my carry-on; a guard
stops me, unrolls my socks, and there it is,
a threat to national security. How can I
travel this way, bereft even of longing?
I do it anyway; I climb rickety stairs, avoiding
the Barbie-glazed gaze of the stewardess
and the winks of be-suited Priority Passenger
2A, who's on his second drink. I think
of my ubiquitous wish: the word *gay* scrawled
with tasteful lucidity in pink on either cheek.
To hell with sexual fluidity; I'm travelling to meet
you, but the you I love's already gone. I predict
an automaton; indeed, your father takes my bag
while you slur behind, reading trashy mags.

For a week's worth of mornings, I slump
at your parents' breakfast nook, perforating
waffles, wanting you in this frumpy haven
as much as I do in the breezy city where you roll
camp slang like cigarettes, dress in natty suits
because you care to. I won't dare you to speak;
I don't care to. But sweetie—lover—
you'll never cure me; I'll never breeze in and out
of my identity like the storms that haunt
the coast you pace. My face will always be
the beacon in the only shot your parents took:
the two of us two feet apart, you staring
at rocks, brine, gulls, anything but sun.

Memorize men's names to salt conversation.
Memorize caution,

but in spite of everything, they'll guess.
Unacknowledged, like your guest. They'll make
assumptions, but never get the grind quite
right: mowing the lawn, drying dishes,
hanging photos of parents who'll die
without naming their daughter's wishes.
I can't live like this, will never understand
what's so grand about a relation based on
deception. It's love you're after, love we're all
afraid we'll never master. Don't you remember
how it felt the first time we rowed together:
tugging up anchor, striving steadily away
from shore? I admired your arms then, *friend,*
because they courted strength without
hesitation, upsetting the smooth surface of the ocean
with ripples that tongued unrecordable music,
cleaned themselves like cats, then were gone.

Stone

Cupped in your palm, you're sorry
it's dead. You want to stroke it to moan,
but that cleft is no mouth, no pulse
but your own, driven by stone to frustration.
You want it to speak, to tell the story
of every striation—how what melts
below moss becomes coarse and then rougher,
tough and then harder, till flow feels
impossible. You want to lick the sleeper's
spatter-colors, coax fire you'd thought
historical. Instead you skip the stone
over the water and watch it sink, counting
rings you won't answer while I count sheep.

Scratch

Felt doesn't bleed. "Who's solid?"
shifts. To aim for something is to hit
or miss—no way around this.
A woman stretches her arm. Fixes
the pulse of her cue on the shot.
She might find the hole, she might
not. But *close* is just *lose*
when you see what you're missing—
the beautiful math of the studied decision,
the careful extension. Aim, show, risk.
Above the table, harsh lights stay honest;
not every patient green thing grows.

Chaos Festival

Heat lightning knows terrible things.
No rain but beauty, no sound but shape: the jagged cross
that splits the sky into desire. Silver spasms
within and against harsh blue, rippling and cohering again,
eternally new. Minutes ago I broke you; now I want
to keep driving, but you want to pull over and watch
in case lightning holds a clue to what comes next. Split
shimmer comes the silver cross. Once it was your body
I yearned for, reaching inside till you thought you'd split,
my mouth shimmering hours after. Once, but not in this car,
not tonight, after I've told you how little I can give now,
you jerked my hands from the wheel to soothe stark need.
This sky is night's hunger, not ours, not our separation we see
destroying the violet scrim of an infinite light show. No,
you and I are simply audience, intent on turning
present tense to memory quickly, so as to bear it,
history housed like heat in light. Your hands graze
my throat, drawing loss a line above my pulse, my lips
no longer slick but shape, my tongue no longer speed
but sound, my car no longer company but lights
stammering past your window on nights you can't sleep,
but sit up watching heat lightning try and fail
to carve its name across that insubstantial veil.

Choke Season

At seven it drops like a veil. I gape to breathe,
ragweed's authoritarian hands circle my lungs,
and I stammer as if with passion. Eleven,
I turn my head away from you and pray for winter,
snow the sweep that scurries pollen home to sleep.
You call me beautiful as I drift off, but this flush
is only death's preview. I peddle the air
with fish lips, desperate for what floats us.
What crazy trust allows us to sleep entangled
as the moon turns Peeping Tom? I'll never know
how your lungs feel, heavy with dust. Not even lust
can prop our lids open; our eyes veil,
we're inadvertently coy, invisible as when we stand
just so, pretending we don't know or notice
the details lovers learn: the way my lashes
slit when my nose tickles, the wheeze you tremble,
the noises we make when we curl together and rock,
content to coil without a brood, becoming our end
of the millennium, more reckless than pollen
because finite, riskier than seasons because less certain,
and you are in my arms only for this generation, no
mirror image of our faces pressing against the window
of our sex. Only when we part the veil that shades us
by walking openly a pair down busy streets
does our love breed, lilting through heavy air like seed.

Lives of Obscure Lesbian Martyrs

At the moment of the miracle, the neon clock
slurred like truck-stop coffee, and her features
took on the spacy peace of a schoolgirl's icon.
Snow buried our cars; she told me later
that I ate through drifts, a human snowblower
with an icy grin. She moved in; we spooned
and loped without spawning, sparking
jealousy among breeder neighbors. They waved
banners, forcing us to become dissenters;
proud of our inadvertent rebellion, we nonetheless
longed for an immaculate conception.

I was certain she could cure the blind—
one encounter with her heavenly beauty
would bring back sight. Days, she was Mary
in her dusk-blue sweater; nights,
a manger animal. That sloe-eyed gaze.
I worshipped readily, never dreaming
a less demanding god would steal her.
Feeling her heart become a calendar,
she waited for the cock to crow
outside our window—signal for a final kiss.
Later, her voice would join the neighbors' hosannas
in the sing-song lilt of the formerly curious.

When I realized she'd cheated on me
over and over, one tryst rolling into another
like the waves I walked when the ocean
was willing, her robe dissolved
in my ready fists. I held her left wrist
to my ear and listened to the breakable bones
that had also done this thing. To knowingly
hurt someone is to believe oneself a god.
Is it any wonder that I cleansed
and swaddled her dead intentions?
But the body we ate was my body, the blood
mine, and every miracle, and every night
we spent together was a parable.

Left to ponder hermeneutics,
I searched the scene for every relic—
a single hair clinging to the soap dish,
a photograph taken at the Christmas party
where she sat showing off her legs,
a grocery list with SLIMFAST in big print—
I took all these things, and matches,
and went into the wilderness alone.
I let the first match lick my finger,
watched it blacken, felt the burn travel,
becoming historical. Then I lit the stash
and breathed the smoke greedily, incorporating
martyrdom into the chapters of my body.

Bound

Walking home from the grocery, my wrists bound by plastic bag bracelets, I saw my cat Chloe luxuriating on the stoop. Two blocks closer and Chloe became a thin white package wound twice with tape, addressed to the previous tenant, a stranger to me. I set the package on the table while I put away the milk, then worked a little longer on the letter I'd been writing since my ex told me about Marlene.

Without AC the kitchen was steamy, but a few hours later the carpet bled early winter: white flakes everywhere, the package shredded. I wanted to chide Chloe, but you can't punish an animal after her bad deeds are over. Instead I shook Kibbles into her bowl to cover the startled mouse staring up at the ceiling. Chloe clawed her thanks, which sent me back to my letter with a really good line about how my pain was like a bracelet, only not a diamond bracelet like the one my father gave my mother for their engagement, but handcuffs. My ex had the key; if she'd write back, maybe I could unlock the clasp, maybe I could understand the pain she'd caused me— Marlene, but also those lies about Nancy and that crazy fight in Sears. Our last dialogue was really criss-crossed monologues on our machines; when she used the word *hate*, it rang false, her tone sensual, savoring its impact. I felt strangled, which I decided to put in the letter—*strangled* is a strong word, like *snow*, which hadn't melted as I'd half-hoped.

The package lay face-down; I turned it over, thinking to re-package it *return to sender*, but the address was gone, and some of the cover of the magazine inside, though I could still make out the woman's expression, shards of pleasure broken over surprise, and her wrists, bound between her breasts. I drank a cup of coffee before giving in to curiosity. Inside were photos of women together, their expressions like the cover model's: longing lurking alongside astonishment and fear, as if they'd just realized that what was happening was what they'd been bred for. I picked up the other magazines spilling from the torn wrapper, tossed them in the trash, and washed my hands. Then I went back to my letter, which was nearly finished, and then it was.

I re-read it. There were some good lines; I knew it would make my ex furious. Through darkness, Chloe glowed on the stoop as I walked outside to bury the letter in my mailbox. I had to tug hard on the tiny door to unlock the clasp.

Then the open mouth.

Then the red flag, meaning *stop*.

Then the inevitable delay.

Whiteout

Amnesia's unnatural; even the cedar remembers winter.
Today's calendar square gleams cream: erasure or open palm?
I woke this morning older than I ever thought I would be.
Anniversary: if we were speaking, she'd describe the gash
wind tore through storm's scrim, forget the story of me
digging her car out with bare hands. This year the cold
is louder than her absence, softer than apologies stammered
into unwashed sheets. Things I know burrow, invisible
beneath a sameness of small tumbles. Do laden branches
forgive the snow its weight? What I'd give to know
the fallen sparrow clings, visionary, to every last gesture
of its receding flock! She wasn't the first or last.
There are others, lost, like the prayers that escape my lips
when I can't find forgiveness. Always: *strength*. Who will hear
confessions if not the last bird, pariah of the frozen wing,
who'll then rise from snow, thawed by the warmth of a thousand
lips' sorrows? This morning's silence chills me. Silent Iowa
is hell; the sheeted hills show amnesia's what's natural:
sinking to chill, denying the miracle of proximity.

Breath

I called that friend of Marnie's one Saturday because the light
in the living room had burned out and I kept forgetting
to buy a new bulb. We watched half a movie. After sex
I listened to the noises she made in the bathroom
and tried to decide if I wanted her to stay. One circle
around the block with the dog and she seemed to expect it.
I gave her the right side of the bed I'd bought with Donna.
As she drifted off, she pulled the blankets from my feet.

At three-thirty-eight I woke to the sound of her death.
Somehow I knew that the choking gasps she made
filling bad lungs with air were the sounds she'd make
in some far-off or fast-approaching future, stay or go
looming a larger question. The dog followed me as I paced,
searching for medicine, warm towels, whatever you give
someone who can't breathe. I was clueless; air is something
I take for granted. She looked blue. I worried sex had brought it on.

When she mentioned mold, we moved our blankets
into the living room. I forgot about the bulb, snapped it on,
listened to the sputter. She seemed to breathe easier
in the new room. The porch light glowed through the window;
I watched her chest rise and fall as she slept. Then morning,
time to circle the block with the dog, make coffee, gripe
about Marnie: how she was always trying to fix people
up with her exes. Then it was ten, and she drove away.

After Donna came back and left again, after the dog was hit
when she slipped under the fence and ran onto Snow Street,
I thought of gestures I should've made to soothe her scarred
lungs' spasms. But I couldn't call after hearing her death
echo prematurely in the wrong setting. This way I could imagine
a finer bed, a kinder lover cradling her in her arms—
or his, if she was into men—but not her children's,
since neither one of us wanted kids. We knew this,
as we knew, without words, that I'd be the one to regret it.

Forgiveness Finds Me at the Agawam

Driving back to Boston from Gloucester
I let myself meander, the way we got into
that mess in the first place. This time, the roads
loved me. They led me to the Agawam. My shoes cried
sand in the lot of the diner when I tipped them;
the waitress let me snag a booth, Formica
circa 1950, the year my mother turned seven
and decided *two children*. I ate to forget you,
as I'd gone to the sea to re-learn, outside your touch,
a body that knew itself for a quarter century
before we met. In the water, the taste
of your skin faded, replaced by stronger salt.
Froth breaking over me wasn't your skirt;
the burn, invisible at first, had nothing to do
with your hands but was the sun's harsh work,
ordinary as a waitress memorizing orders.
Did she leave the diner so full of recited desires
that she couldn't sleep, but sat by some view's
sill, cursing strangers' gaping mouths? With me
still, though you'd been gone a year: the fear
that every woman was the one you left me for.
I watched her hands, wondering what she liked
to carry—nothing hot or sloppy. Then there I was,
inventing her life for her. I heard you chide me, saw
that scene again: more salt, a fistful of keys.

In dreams you're on your knees; I hover over,
reeling apologies from your lips like wire.
But when I wake there's only this one life,
and the knowledge we might not speak again
in the course of it. Which means *never*.
And never's long. Like, forever. I want to suck
this bitterness from old wrongs, bear it
within me, immunity; I want to re-learn,
outside our history, the generosity once
native to me. To recognize forgiveness
like home's geography. *Take your time,*
the waitress winked; I wanted to kiss her
for the gift you wouldn't give me.
From the window, I watched the sun
bruise as it fell, glinting off the diner:
a car travelling nowhere. Why build a train
without tracks? Even inland, even inside,
the air hung heavy with salt; within me
a storm tossed new tides, forgiveness
buffeting bitterness, wave on wave.
In every booth of the Agawam, passengers
ate to remember, travelling towards
each other. Away from hunger.

Revival

Lord lift me. Once it was enough to sit beneath the tent,
grandmother weeping beside me, fanning her face
with the preacher's CV. That ecstasy
was as real as spring rain, warm jam; my hands
in dreams become birds, fluttering over, leaving
no guilt. Once it was enough to be saved
on Sunday, born again in time for supper.
The preacher knelt before me. Touched my chin.
Liked what he saw, though now when my lover

licks me, I catch myself
wondering *how can a woman bear*
to touch my body? It was to be a new life.
Grandmother promised I would feel it—
a burning within, something very small, hovering
like birds. Birds on the ceiling. Ceiling, stars, snow.
It was as real as winter, burying us in beautiful quilts,
connecting us to a town that would have us burned
at stake even in freezing temperatures, we witches,
our magic real to them and us, real as Christ
spiriting my blood, quickening me, readying me
for Mary's hands. Now when her tongue hovers

inside me before beginning slow circles, I shake so hard
the neighbors upstairs are born again.
In this way we contribute to the spiritual upkeep
of this terrible city, small and without mystery,
dotted with bars and churches, each canceling
the other out. In this way we are reborn
from within and not without, our very bodies a wet
Bible for the millennium. *Swing low, sweet chariot,*

Grandmother sang, paper fluttering like a flirt's wet
lashes, wrists aching after an hour. And over.
Hours and hours. *Sweet ache.* Sweetheart,
what is passion for, if not to worship
the body, split-steaming in snow? I want nothing
more than redemption when I take you, Sweetheart,
sweet ache, two fingers, my whole arm burning

as if to break. It was to be a new life, love
without a country, country without wives,
Mary without Jesus, God, or the beautiful animals
who licked her thighs as she gave birth, they alone
thinking to bring a gift she could use: solace,
the promise that pain and this life are only temporary.

IV

I smile at us, two beautiful girls in the mirror, and ignore the scent of burning flesh.
J.T. LeRoy, "Baby Doll"

Love Is a Map I Must Not Set on Fire

When I take you in flurries, the lights go out.
Stars come out. You come out again.
Love is under the bed, a children's monster.
The dildo gleams. We hold knives in our hands.

When I take you in words, we reinvent categories.
Chair is a particular type of chair.
There are no abstractions; we are all specifics.
The window gleams, awash with stars.

When I take you home, all hardwood is sacred.
The things we buy represent nothing but use.
Kiwis gleam; we light them as candles.
The dildo emerges from the dishwasher in time.

When I take you with rings, my fingers simmer.
Together we strangle the ghosts of old loves.
No one comes near the feast of our struggles.
You twirl your fork in my tangled hair.

When I take you with wind beneath terrible branches,
you whirl your skirts to make up for lost time.
You become weather and I am your weatherman.
I point to the map I must not set on fire.

When I take you in marriage, old laws turn to tangles.
You toss your breasts in my face like runes.
When we lie, we say *monster*, a verb in the making.
I must not commit arson. All gleaming is gone.

My Vocation

I love *forensic medicine*, the white jut of bone
tickling my palm, bodies littering the table like scarves.
Or is it *forestry?* I can never remember which word
came to me in sleep, spoken like one of the commandments,
saving me from a lifetime spent xeroxing autographs.

Once, someone I loved lunged for my throat.
Once, someone I loved kept a bird beneath her sweater.
What she was after was the feel of life
denied access to air. What I got was my vocation,
gasping for help, for myself or something winged.

Love comes to me, and leaves. Even that certainty recedes,
like each one of the commandments, saving me
from a lifetime spent following white wings.
My vocation's a voice, snared inside a woman's throat:
each aptitude notes, rung through flesh, rung through bone.

Tell Me More Why

Because her face is green in the painting
but it's still her face. Because the pages
go quickly. Because my hand shakes
when you do that but I can't talk about it.
Even as a child I told lies to get people
to pass the salt. It always worked.
I start to say one thing and it turns
into another, something more
beautiful. I want to feed it and brush it:
grey fur. Nothing so simple as *secrecy*.
Nothing so simple as *their language*.
Because I like the sound of words
done over and over the same way—*clay*
clay clay or even *carve carve carve*—more
and more like music. Nothing so simple as
our era. Because stories are ugly
and the world doesn't work that way. Because
tray rhymes, and that tray can carry
bread with honey, newly sharpened knives.

Night Music

All night long, the forks.
The sequence of coffees treating
my arms as if they felt like hers.
Don't say it wasn't honest: each table
spoke, a spirit split by language
into several selves. Underneath
loomed an occasional solitude;
bugs crept, and light.
We went beyond, until the forks
sang *do wah diddy,*
like heterosexual men
worshipping a living Barbie.
Each spirit questioned, asking
can you be with this one
or is it merely coincidence, I guess
meaning the way the diner
held us both, and outside on the pave:
two cars, parked almost parallel.
It wasn't negligence,
exactly; rather, *our hands pooled*
like water pouring into water
and what happened after
was advertised like scenery,
each kiss parading in drag,
singing nought but the refrain,
do wah diddy, as if gossiping
about all that would eventually happen.

At Bar

The egg tree quivers with joy. Across the bar,
the blonde in the thin white sweater lights a fire
and rolls her eyes. Her laugh is a bray;
her dinner *pommes frites* and olives. She breaks open

an egg, salts carefully. Three tall men enter laughing.
They down shots. *Simpatico* bartender wipes the rim
of a new glass with his whites; sweater lady eats,
tells life story. At the bar's far edge sits a couple

with mats at their places. They swap sips, salads,
and fishes. He tosses a roll, explaining. Her back
is to the wall; she is learning. The late crowd is coming:
much black, black crowding

the walls' green trim, brushing past the lady
with olives and eggs. She drops money,
steps out onto a deserted street. The night crowd
takes its own coat and is seated.

The Limbo Queen

Heading for the party with potato chips
and a bottle of something.
Arriving, trying to find the sway
of the swing that's already in motion.

Beer, *und so weiter.* On the bookshelves:
Joyce, *The Joy*, a couple of photographs.
At my elbow a boy,
bending to hear above Harry Belafonte.

Awkwardly talking.
Taking an interest in pauses that stagger.
Awkwardly dancing: jamming,
and gnashing, and physically bragging.

Stars on the patio,
out of range of the radio.
Sharing one curve
of a crack in the granite.

Closing my eyes
on the garden, your glasses.
Shaking the twigs from the furls
of our dresses.

First Fist

Never enough of orange or the rest of light.
Rest your head on my mortal shoulder.
Time stretches between us sheer as a cat.
In the coil of hair and its mystery I lay my head.
Anyway, the clock doesn't know your name
or the date of your death. Birth me again
in the wounds of your sweater. Sweeter
the second time and those thereafter.

Aftermath

This is a flammable letter set to music only we can hear. Do you hear *we*. Do you hear stretches of solitude and a glimpse of the racetrack. If I carry you with me. If albatross. If gloss familiar. Birds on every corkscrew in Seattle and on the wire a burnt crow the size of a bar code's half-sister. Do you hear *miss her*. A record crackling, unprepared for sampling and white girls worshipping rap. Will you set this note on fire. Will you Lindy Hop with the Mac Daddy of SoDo. First pleasure, then aftermath in the shape of a fissure. After *yes* there is no intermission.

Elegy

The clock's light scissoring her forehead,
the tape stuck on the same arpeggio, and outside
the collie at the spaniel's throat.
She replaces the concerto. Traces of snow,
three cyclists, lawn ornaments.
Or maybe water: I can't remember
whether we were over ocean
when she reached for my book
and snapped it shut. Maybe the refrain was a bird,
calling the shore by name.
Even with her head bent towards me,
she was taller: a fish leaping,
and then the catch. Nothing to do but count
as the temperature dropped,
snow became ornament, the dog's throat
opened, and the clock's lawn stopped.

Early Erasures

Send forth colors. I'm butch before lift-off.
After that I batten back. Say good-bye to my face
or suffer the strifes of ten thousand saints,
spokes tinted to the taste of the Catherine wheel.
Fingernail polish dries in the wind on the hand
riding waves out the window. I let you go.
The sound is the shape of a hand, meaning *stop*.
In the time of erasure there is no touch.
On the edge of an unwanted autograph
I hang the hat Belonging wore. We wore, then were,
then wore down. Hang any flag over the autobahn.
Wait for an election to study bones, each chad
ambiguous as a civil union. Who wins the execution
if the machine misfires, if good-bye goes unsaid?
In the flesh tree is the guardian of winter.
Flush with the future comes the double-edged razor.
Silence is abuse in the context of scarves, of Juarez,
of white girls starving to seduce Prince Charming.
Rattle-tag trees, even, burn to speak. Topics:
oppression, repression, any -ion left lying around
after the divorce. Sweat clings to the neck
beneath the necklace of you. There's a war on.
It will moan in the desert. You will eat
dessert second. You will Have a Nice Day.

If We Speak Again, It Will Be in Passing

Cat as crucifix hampers the bed, crumbs from last night's sugar-free cookies
in crevices. Says Dog #2: Earthquakes brew beneath the fault lines of Admiral
Hill. Says Post-It: Take down paintings. Cat dries its wings on the rim of my
noose. In other news the next president will be metrosexual, Morse code dashes
for pinstripes in his double-breasted. Therefore. Meaning. What Was. Treed.
It was reminiscent of summer, I mean catching you under the weight of another.
Our hippie reconciliation dried up with the garden, longing for rain that
turned out to be salt. EMPLOYEES MUST WASH HANDS BEFORE
RETURNING TO WORK. The blue woman emerging from the skirts of my
bed turns tourist attraction as my fist blooms inside her. She isn't an ex nor is
she an option. Dog #1 mimics my diction. If we meet again, the Ballard Bridge
will split open for our tug to pass, a giant wife giving directions to a husband
who never asks. You'll be more beautiful. I'll be mathematical. Tremors will cease
and no one will win.

Sunset Language

Don't come to me
with your hair cut short
shorn
at your feet
a tangle of nettles
The moon's undone
and I'm undone with her
craw in the sky
my words clawing my throat
Don't come to me
unless you'll stay
long enough
to say what really happened
ink on your fingers
from the sunset language
heat for an apron
hills in your hair
Don't come to me
Don't speak
Don't break
sun at your back
my back for a shadow
This is what love
This is what love
This is what love
under wartime is like

Dissolve Me

Circus animals at the doorstep
and you, arriving late.
Bandaged, damaged.
How much I—over. Winter.
House of hothouse flowers.
Hats for company. Your swollen arm.

Taking my hand
in the teeth of your hook.
Too late, too late
your photograph dissolves
positive to negative
and back again.

Rowing towards the wreck
in our three-armed boat.
Bruise Bay chilly as a three-dog night.
Fog off Fairhaven. Lost to shore.
That night I would have
taken. Everything. Off
again, on, our lips
locked for the camera. Lost.

I see the sound of the oars
paused above the mirror of winter.

Chihuly Rose

What is broken in you will be whole again
in the half-light where you turn away
from the gun and the vermilion fantasy of the gun
Where you imagine a woman's mouth
creating within you a room of high ceilings
room of windows and doors opening
gate squeaking in a language
you thought no one would master
Late August, and the Chihuly rose
blossoms honey-gold into molten glass
And you as a child, all red hair and fire,
no one to teach you what you needed to know
    how to pour glass without sand walls shattering
    how to lace shoes with one hand and a hook
You in the dirt, you making glass,
breaking glass, breaking down, breaking
the things you love most
    gates
    bones
    language
because that is what you do with one hand
In the fantasy of the woman's mouth
fire drips from your shears and hardens to ice
Remember acetylene blackening the positive
the ladle sighing in water after
Remember your hook pressed to her hip
disabling the molten hands of the clock

Top

Look. There is the lost (not toy but) *time*—
the small cowlicked tomboy spinning
something magical with a string and a *flick*.
Later, she will use her wrists
to enter women more beautiful even
than spinning tops—spinners of lives,
lies, children, and documents.
We must document this, you and I—
two women who've not forgotten
the thin thread that begins *motion*,
that becomes *wobble*, finally fall—
our fall, fully chosen, from the lives
we were given. *Flick*.
Do let go. Do let the string do what it will.
Flaunt the top, teetering above the sidewalk,
uncertain how long its gleam will last;
flaunt the wrists, and the tiny toy, and the time
it took to get here: shedding sparks, spinning,
not wanting anything. Not even childhood;
not even children. Document *whir*.
We were born to this. Fall tops summer;
summer comes *over and over*. It will find us.

About the Author

CAROL GUESS is the author of *Seeing Dell, Switch,* and *Gaslight.* Her novel *Switch* was a finalist for the ALA Gay Lesbian Bisexual Transgender Book Award; her memoir *Gaslight* was a finalist for a Lambda Literary Award. She teaches at Western Washington University and lives in Seattle. She has a B.A. from Columbia University and an M.F.A. from Indiana University.

Colophon

The body text is composed in Adobe Caslon with titles in Overexposed. Page composition was completed by ImPrint Services, Corvallis, Oregon.